Changing State

By the end of this book you will know more about:

- Different states of matter.
- How materials change from one state to another.
- The water cycle.

You will:

- Plan and carry out a fair test about evaporation.
- Measure temperature.
- Interpret data.
- Draw line graphs.

Task 1

What do the words mean?

- Look at these words describing the state of materials and changes that can happen to them.

melting

evaporating

condensing

boiling

freezing

solidifying

- Write down and describe what you think each word means.
- How confident are you with your description? Read the key below and write a number from 1 to 3 beside each of your descriptions.

Key

1 = I'm just guessing – I don't really know the meaning.

2 = I think I know the meaning, but I'm not quite sure.

3 = I'm sure I know the meaning.

When a liquid evaporates it becomes a gas. Liquids other than water evaporate.

Task 2

Wet and dry

All these pictures show liquids evaporating.

Discuss these questions.

Can you think of any other examples of liquids evaporating?

What has happened to the liquid in each picture? Where does it go?

What do you think would make a liquid evaporate more quickly?

When some of these liquids evaporate, there is a smell. Why?

Make careful measurements and record them in a table and graph.

Task 3

Scientific Enquiry

Investigating evaporation

1,2

You need:

- measuring cylinders
- containers of water
- thermometer
- fan

If you put some water in an open container, it will evaporate.

- Work in a group. What do you think might make a difference to how much water evaporates over two days?
- Choose one thing to change – one thing that your group will investigate.
- How will you know how much water has evaporated? Use Task Sheet 1 to plan your investigation.
- Check your plans with your teacher before carrying out your investigation.

- Measure the volumes of water carefully. Use Task Sheet 2 to record your results.
- What type of graph will you draw? Will it be a bar chart or a line graph?
- Describe the pattern on your graph. What do your results tell you about evaporation? Explain why you think this happens.

Relate patterns in results to scientific knowledge.

Task 4

Scientific Enquiry

Drying sponges

3

Zaheera and her class were investigating evaporation. Zaheera told her class about something she had noticed at home.

Read the web pages.

1

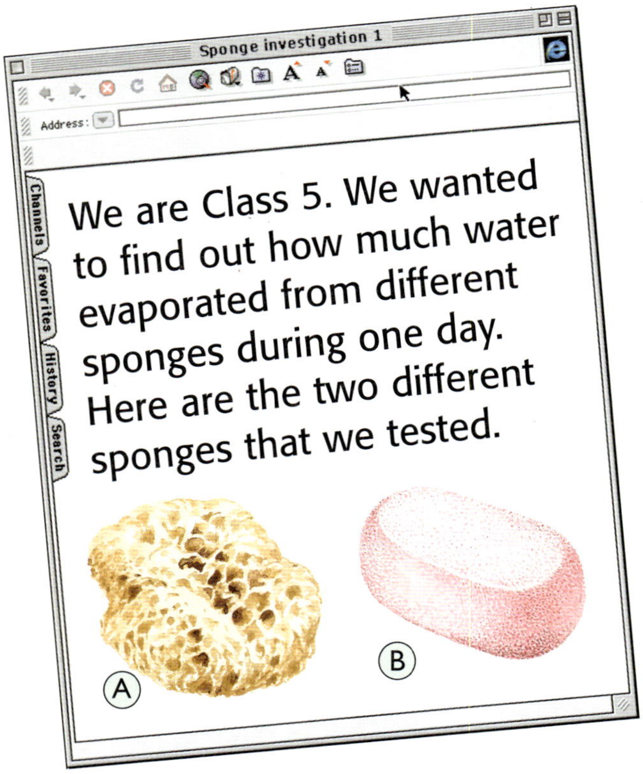

2

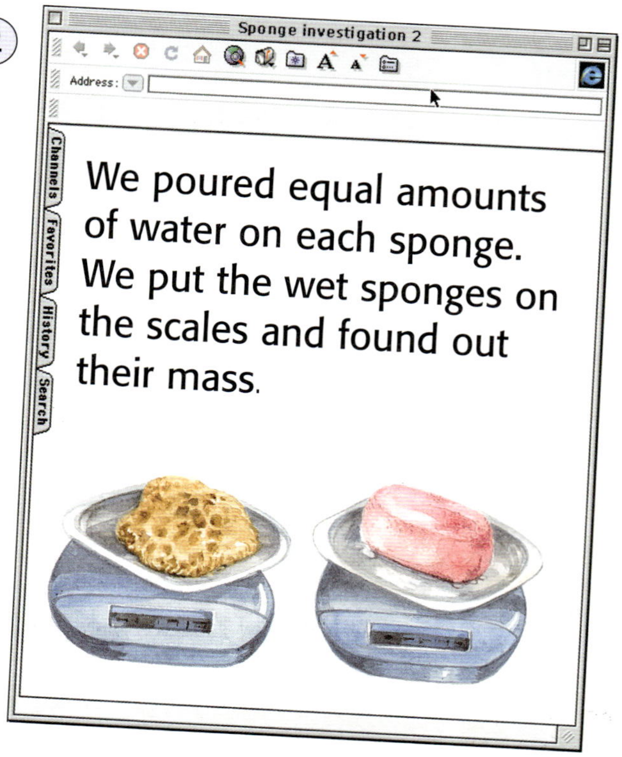

3

Sponge investigation 3

We checked their mass every hour. The mass went down because some of the water had evaporated.
We worked out how much water had evaporated.

4

Sponge investigation 4

Here are two graphs. They show what happened to the water on our sponges during the day.

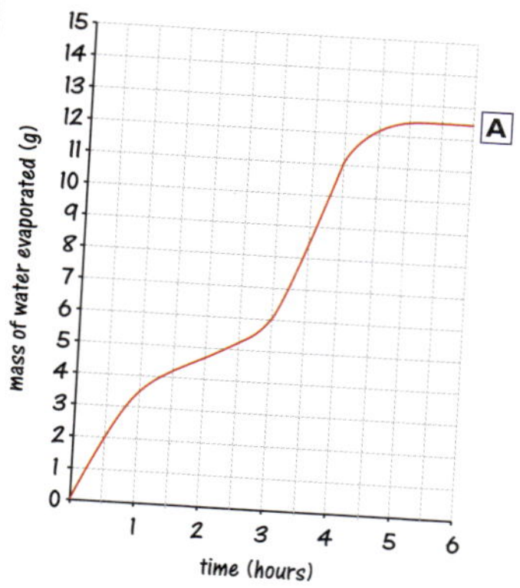

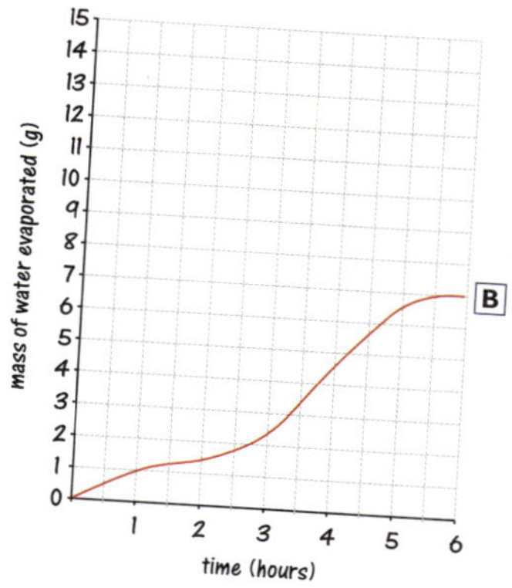

5

Sponge investigation 5

If you put both graphs on the same piece of paper, this is what it looks like.

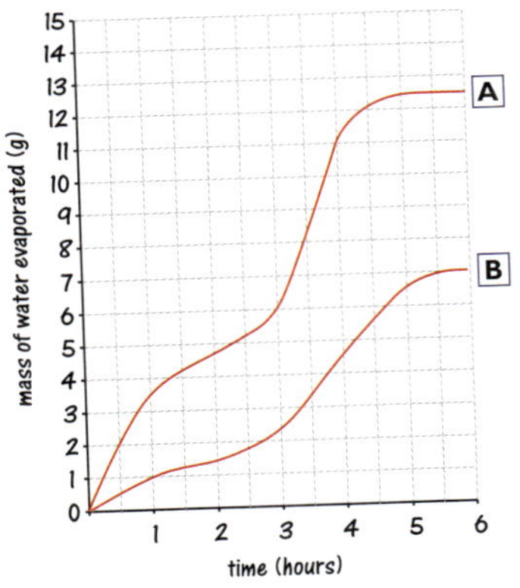

- Complete Task Sheet 3.

Extra Challenge

- In your group find some different sponges and try Class 5's investigation.
- Create a web page to show your results.

Everyday appliances can speed up evaporation.

Task 5 Drying off

- Look at these pictures of everyday appliances. Each one is designed to speed up the evaporation of water.

- Make a poster advertising one of these appliances. Explain how it makes water evaporate more quickly.
- You could design your poster using a computer and include digital photographs.

Dries faster than ever because...

A drying sensation...

Tested by scientists...

Condensation is when a gas changes into a liquid.

Task 6

Scientific Enquiry

Dripping drops

You need:

- transparent bowl
- hand-hot water
- cling film
- ice cubes

- Study the picture below and set up the experiment.
  Make sure that there are no holes in the cling film and that that no water can get through it.

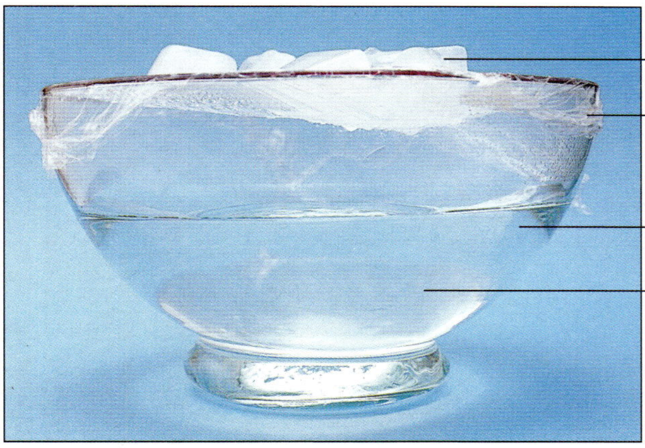

- Watch carefully and then draw and write to describe what is happening.

- Discuss these questions.

- Copy and complete these sentences.

1 I think the drops of water came from…

2 I think some drops are larger than others because…

3 I think the drops of water will stop forming when…

Fact File

Condensation and evaporation

When a gas cools, it turns into a liquid. This process is called **condensation**. It is the opposite process to **evaporation**.

Evaporation

Condensation

Water vapour in the air may condense when it meets a cold surface.

Task 7

Condensation and evaporation

4

- Look at the pictures and think about these questions.
  - When does water vapour condense and become liquid water?
  - When does liquid water evaporate and become water vapour?
- Write down your answers on Task Sheet 4.

Words to learn and use:
appliance
condensation
evaporation
reversible
water vapour

- When changes can go backwards and forwards we call them **reversible** changes. Do you think evaporation and condensation are reversible changes? Why?

When a liquid boils it changes into a gas.
Water boils at 100°C.
Make a prediction and decide whether the evidence supports it.

Task 8

Scientific Enquiry

It's boiling hot!

5,6

Jon and Natalie are cooking a surprise birthday meal for their friend Emily.

"Emily will be home soon," says Natalie.

"Oh no!" says Jon. "We've forgotten to cook the potatoes."

"Quick, we must boil them now, they take ages to cook," cries Natalie.

Jon and Natalie quickly wash and peel the potatoes, put them in a saucepan of cold water and put them on the cooker.

"Don't forget to turn the heat down when the water starts to boil," says Nat.

"Nat, have you gone mad?" asks Jon. "We want the potatoes to cook quickly. I'm going to leave the heat turned up high the whole time. That way the water will boil and go on getting hotter and hotter and they'll cook much faster."

What do you think? Should Jon leave the cooker turned up high once the water starts boiling? Will that make the water get hotter and hotter?

Imagine that you are heating a pan of tap water on a cooker and taking the temperature of the water with a thermometer every two minutes until after the water has boiled.

- What would a graph of your results look like?
- Make a prediction. Draw a line graph like this one and sketch how you think the line would continue.

- Find out what really happens. Use the results in Task Sheet 5 or record the results as your teacher does this experiment.
- Plot a line graph of results on Task Sheet 6 or use a computer.
- Does your line graph look like your prediction?
- Use your graph to answer these questions.

1 At what temperature does water boil?

2 Once liquid water has boiled, can it get any hotter?

3 What happens to liquid water when it boils?

4 If you left a pan of water boiling for a long time, what would happen? Why?

5 How are evaporation and boiling the same?

6 How are evaporation and boiling different?

Measure temperature and make careful observations.

Task 9

Scientific Enquiry

Icy water

7

You need:

- beaker
- temperature sensor or a thermometer
- water
- small ice cubes
- clock, watch or timer
- spoon or stirrer

- Put about 50 cm^3 of water in a beaker. Add several small ice cubes.
- Stir the water and ice cubes and measure the temperature. Repeat this every 10 minutes for about two hours.

- Use Task Sheet 7 to record your results and plot a line graph. You could draw your graph using a computer.
- As you plot each point, predict where the next point will be. How close to your results were your predictions?
- What do you think is the temperature of your classroom? How can you tell?

Greenside School is a large primary school. There are three Year 5 classes.

Class 5a works in the old part of the school. It has a few windows that are high up. Not much sunlight comes into 5a's classroom and it can be quite chilly.

Class 5b has a room in the new extension. This is a modern building. It gets some warm sunlight in the morning but none after lunch.

Class 5c works in a classroom on the other side of the playground. It has big windows down both sides. It gets lots of sunshine in the morning and afternoon and is very warm and cosy.

After lunch, one sunny afternoon all three Year 5 classes carried out the icy water experiment. They all used the same amount of water and the same number of ice cubes. They had good thermometers and they measured the temperature carefully but their results were not quite the same.

- Why do you think this happened?
- Sketch what you think the line graphs from each class would look like on a graph like this one.
- Use a different colour line for each class.

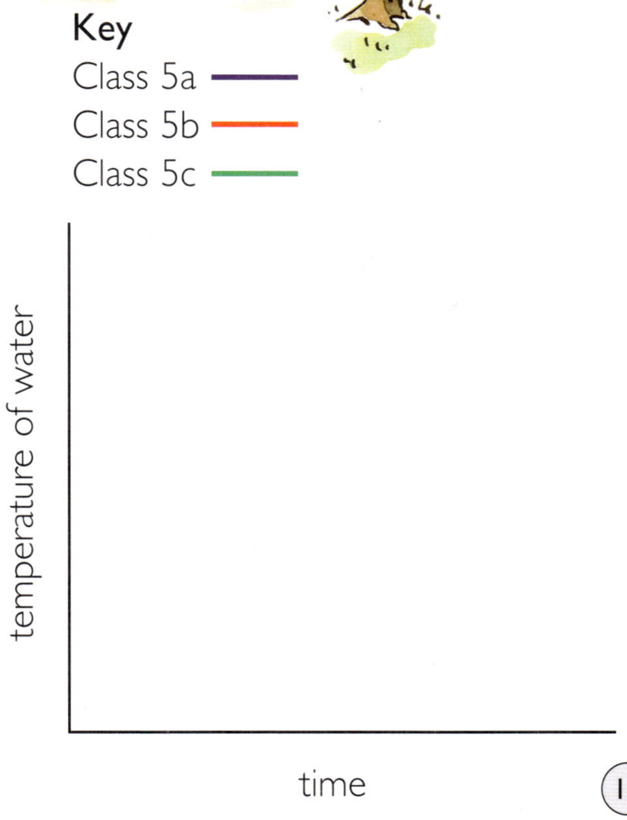

Materials can be in one of three states – solid, liquid or gas.

Task 10

Changing state

8

At normal everyday temperatures, materials are in their solid state, their liquid state or their gas state. If we change the temperature and make materials hotter or colder, they can change state.

Use these words to complete the concept map on Task Sheet 8.

Words to learn and use:
boil
freeze
melt
solidify

Task 11

The Changing State Game

a

Read about how to play the Changing State Game.
Cut out the cards on Task Sheet 9 to play the game.

freeze

condense

evaporate

solidify

melt

boil

The playground is divided into three zones marked 'solid', 'liquid' and 'gas'.

Everyone starts by standing in the zone marked 'liquid'.

Your teacher picks out a card. In this case the word on the card is 'evaporate'. Liquids can evaporate and change into a gas.

Everyone runs to the 'gas' zone. The last one to get there is out.

Your teacher calls out another word. The word on the card is 'boil'. Gases can't boil.

Everyone has to stay in the 'gas' zone. If anyone runs, they are out too.

Play the game until there is a winner or until everyone is tired!

Fact File

The Water Cycle

You have been learning about two processes called **evaporation** and **condensation**.

These processes are an important part of the **water cycle**.

Water evaporates from lakes and **oceans** and changes into water vapour. The water vapour rises into the air. As it goes higher it gets colder and forms **clouds**.
When it is cooled enough the water vapour changes from a gas back into a liquid and falls as rain and snow. It is carried back to the oceans by rivers and streams and the cycle continues.

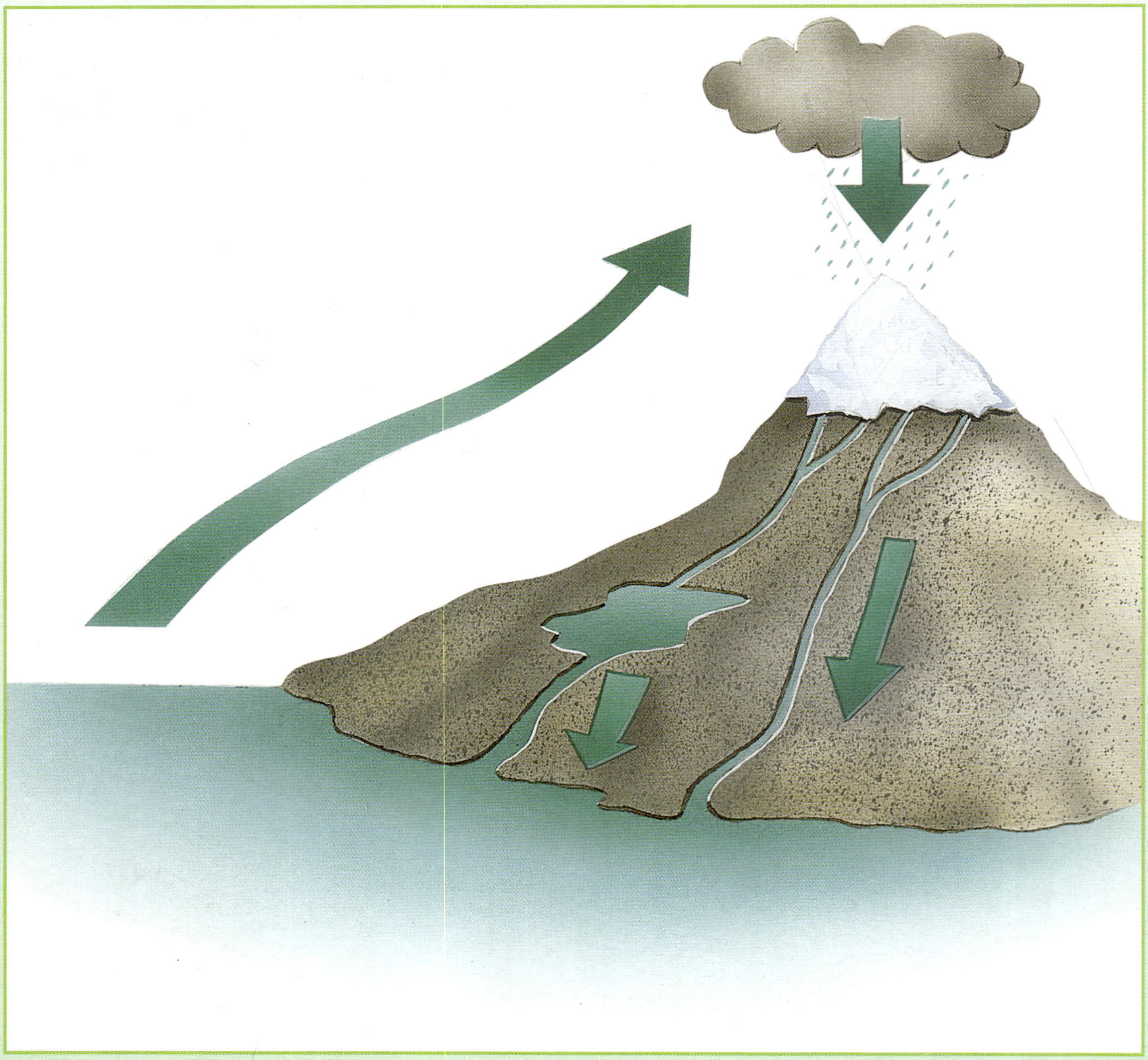

Water evaporates from lakes and oceans, condenses into clouds and eventually falls as rain or snow. This is the water cycle.

Task 12

Thinking about the water cycle

These children are asking questions about the water cycle.

- How would you answer their questions? Talk about it with a partner. Write down your answers.
- Compare your answers with other groups.

Words to learn and use:
cloud
ocean
vapour

Task 13

Play the water cycle game

Design a game like this one that shows how the water cycle works. You could use drawing software to help you.

ounter
art.
first
a
cle.
hrow
nish.

Checkpoint

A day of changing states

10

This is the start of Sam's day.

- Why do you think Sam has underlined some parts? Why has Sam written a letter beside the underlined sections?

- Use Task Sheet 10 to read the rest of Sam's story and identify all the changes of state described. Use this key to help you.

Key

B = boiling
C = condensing
E = evaporating
F = freezing
M = melting
S = solidifying

Write a story about your day. Put in as many changes of state as you can. Underline each one and write a letter beside it to show which change of state is happening.

> I woke up and went to the bathroom. The mirror was dirty so I breathed on it. It went all misty(C) so I rubbed it clean. I looked out of the window. It had been raining and there were puddles everywhere, but the sun was now out and they were drying up(E).

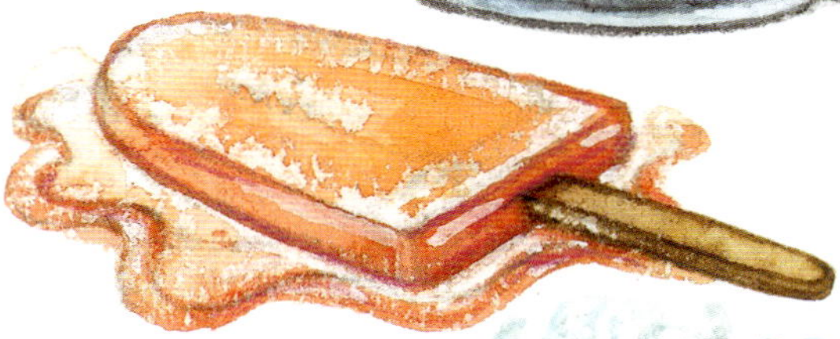

Summary

Which of these do you know and which can you do?

- I know that when a liquid evaporates it becomes a gas.
- I know that liquids other than water evaporate.
- I can make careful measurements and record them in a table and graph.
- I can relate patterns in results to scientific knowledge.
- I know that everyday appliances can speed up evaporation.
- I know that condensation is when a gas changes into a liquid.
- I know that condensation is the reverse of evaporation.
- I know that water vapour in the air may condense when it meets a cold surface.
- I know that when a liquid boils it changes into a gas.
- I know that water boils at 100°C.
- I can make a prediction and decide whether the evidence supports it.
- I can measure temperature and make careful observations.
- I know that materials can be in one of three states – solid, liquid or gas.
- I know what happens in the water cycle.

Complete your **Science Log** to show how well you know these and how well you can do them. Circle a face for each statement.

Glossary

melting

boil – when a liquid changes into a gas at a particular temperature.

changing state – when a liquid changes to a solid or gas or when a gas or solid changes to a liquid. It is a reversible change.

evaporation – when a liquid changes into a gas. It can happen over a range of temperatures.

freeze – when a material changes from a liquid to a solid at a cold temperature such as in a freezer.

gas – a material in a form that flows easily and can change shape and volume.

liquid – a material in a form that flows and can change shape. Its volume stays the same.

melting – when a material changes from a solid to a liquid.

solid – a material in a form that keeps its shape and volume.

solidify – when a material changes from a liquid to a solid.

state – materials can be in one of three states: solid, liquid or gas.

temperature – a measure of how hot or cold something is.

volume – the amount of space something takes up.

water cycle – when water evaporates from oceans seas and lakes, condenses as clouds and eventually falls as rain.

evaporation